CHOOSING LIFE

OVERCOMING SUICIDE

UNLESS OTHERWISE INDICATED, ALL SCRIPTURE QUOTATIONS ARE TAKEN FROM THE HOLY BIBLE, NEW INTERNATIONAL VERSION ®, NIV ® COPYRIGHT © 1973, 1978, 1984, 2011 BY BIBLICA, INC ™. USED BY PERMISSION. ALL RIGHTS RESERVED WORLDWIDE.

THE USE OF SELECTED REFERENCES FROM VARIOUS VERSIONS OF THE BIBLE IN THIS PUBLICATION DOES NOT NECESSARILY IMPLY PUBLISHER ENDORSEMENT OF THE VERSIONS IN THEIR ENTIRETY.

CHOOSING LIFE, OVERCOMING SUICIDE

COPYRIGHT © 2025 BY CALLI GREENE

802 E AVENUE D, COPPERAS COVE, TX 76522

ISBN: 979-8-218-59750-4

ALL RIGHTS RESERVED. NO PART OF THIS PUBLICATION MAY BE REPRODUCED, STORED IN A RETRIEVAL SYSTEM, OR TRANSMITTED IN ANY FORM OR BY ANY MEANS—ELECTRONIC, MECHANICAL, DIGITAL, PHOTOCOPY, RECORDING, OR ANY OTHER—EXCEPT FOR BRIEF QUOTATIONS IN PRINTED REVIEWS, WITHOUT THE PRIOR PERMISSION OF THE PUBLISHER.

ANY INTERNET ADDRESSES, COMPANY, OR PRODUCT INFORMATION PRINTED IN THIS BOOK ARE OFFERED AS A RESOURCE AND ARE NOT INTENDED TO IMPLY AN ENDORSEMENT BY CALLI GREENE, NOR DOES CALLI GREENE VOUCH FOR THE EXISTENCE, CONTENT, OR SERVICES OF THESE SITES, COMPANIES, OR PRODUCTS BEYOND THE LIFE OF THIS BOOK.

PRINTED IN THE UNITED STATES OF AMERICA.

Disclaimer:

This book contains a personal account of the author's journey through and beyond suicidal thoughts, grounded in their Christian faith and personal relationship with Jesus Christ. The experiences and perspectives shared are deeply personal and are not intended to serve as a substitute for professional mental health care.

If you or someone you know is struggling with suicidal thoughts, please seek help from a qualified mental health professional. You are not alone, and support is available. In the United States, you can contact the Suicide and Crisis Lifeline (simply dial #988), available 24/7.

The inclusion of personal experiences with mental health challenges is intended to foster understanding and hope, not to promote a particular course of action. Every person's journey is unique, and what worked for the author may not be appropriate for others.

This book is dedicated to all who continue to choose life each day.

Author's Note:

My heart grieves deeply for those who have lost a loved one to suicide. My prayer for the remaining family members and friends is for God's love and tenderness to wash over you. May you be the hands and feet of Jesus to help others through your experiences. For those still fighting, thank you for choosing life. I am proud of you. This is a uniquely challenging journey. Keep fighting! Allow your heart to receive God's love because He loves you so much and desires you to be free.

May this book serve as a guide to help those currently struggling with suicidal thoughts understand how to fight suicide with Jesus. Throughout this book, each section includes biblical stories, Rhema words, and scripture references. The Bible stories explored in this guide offer short accounts that illustrate how God loves and interacts with His people. These stories help us learn more about who God is, how He sees us, and how we can live in Him. You will notice that after each Bible story, there's something called a Rhema word. Rhema is Greek for "a spoken word," referring to the spoken or personally applied word of God (Hagin). These words demonstrate the personal and alive nature of God's word. Simply put, Rhema words provide language for when you read a Bible verse or hear something from God, and it speaks directly to your situation and feels like it's meant just for you. After reflecting on each passage of scripture in this book, the Lord shared Rhema words with me, which I will share with you.

Throughout each chapter, you will notice scripture references, which are like addresses for specific Bible verses so that you can find them easily. You will first see the name of the book, followed by the chapter number, and finally the verse number. As an example, if you see John 3:16, John is the name of the book, 3 is the chapter, and 16 is the verse. The end of this book provides additional resources, including prayers, books by other authors, and additional scripture references.

My prayer is that everyone reading this book would be washed in God's love. May your heart be open to receive God in ways you have never experienced before. May your faith grow to believe that by the sacrifice and resurrection of Jesus Christ, we are healed (Isaiah 53:5).

ACKNOWLEDGEMENTS

Gratitude:

    I am incredibly grateful to my loving husband for his support during my writing process. Thank you, Joel, for encouraging me to stand on God's instructions and for holding me accountable to see this project through to the end. To my parents and siblings, thank you for continuing to grow in faith and love each day. Thank you to my excellent Christian counselor, Dr. Pamela Thompson, for helping me see and grow in the Holy Spirit. To Choosing Life's reviewer, and our mentor, Reverend Dr. Angelia Pounds, thank you for walking with us during this journey. Your wisdom and feedback ensured this project could properly reflect biblical truth for God's people. To our editor, Jan Levin, thank you for your diligence in ensuring the words expressed here could be understood by all who may come across this book for generations to come.

An Honest Acknowledgement:

I will never be able to encompass the vastness of suicide and depression. I admit that I will never be able to do justice in explaining in full how and why God acts in certain ways. I desire to express the depth in which He loves you, but I know I'll never be able to encapsulate that because He loves you more than any of us can fully comprehend. Any breakthrough you receive from this book will not be because of me but because you chose to allow Jesus Christ to touch your heart. He wants to be with you. He is eager for you to invite Him in. He desires a willing heart.

Portions of this book may be challenging to read because they will require that we consider and compare our experiences, generational issues, and personal actions with biblical truth as they pertain to suicide and depression. My personal experiences in this area qualify me to speak from my testimony and share my discoveries about the nature and patterns of the spirit of suicide.

I acknowledge that my experiences are not and will never fully encompass anyone else's experiences. However, I know that God brought me to discoveries based on His biblical truth and principles; I encourage everyone to take what I say and judge it against God's word. I will share the strategies God taught me, but remember that God *is* God and will move how He wants to. Thus, your healing journey may differ from mine and require different things. The point is that we look to Him for healing through this journey.

I genuinely believe that you were given your story to share in the timing that God is leading you to share it. Now, I choose to share how God healed me with the encouragement and hope that He can heal you, too.

I ask that you posture your heart to receive so that you may gain the skills to fight and defeat suicide and depression in the spiritual realm.

TABLE OF CONTENTS

TESTIMONY 12

HOW THE SPIRITUAL WORLD OPERATES 24

WHAT IS THE SPIRIT OF SUICIDE? 30

THE HARDEST PART 42

DEPRESSION AND SUICIDAL IDEATIONS IN THE BIBLE 52

HOW TO FIGHT 60

ADDITIONAL RESOURCES 78

TESTIMONY

"Jesus has come to set the captives free"

Luke 4:18 (Paraphrased)

Now Moses was tending the flock of Jethro his father-in-law, the priest of Midian, and he led the flock to the far side of the wilderness and came to Horeb, the mountain of God. There the angel of the Lord appeared to him in flames of fire from within a bush. Moses saw that though the bush was on fire it did not burn up.

So, Moses thought, "I will go over and see this strange sight – why the bush does not burn up."

When the Lord saw that he had gone over to look, God called to him from within the bush, "Moses! Moses!" And Moses said, "Here I am." "Do not come any closer," God said. "Take off your sandals, for the place where you are standing is holy ground."

Then he said, "I am the God of your father, the God of Abraham, the God of Isaac and the God of Jacob." At this, Moses hid his face, because he was afraid to look at God.

The Lord said, "I have indeed seen the misery of my people in Egypt. I have heard them crying out because of their slave drivers, and I am concerned about their suffering. So, I have come down to rescue them from the hand of the Egyptians and to bring them up out of that land into a good and spacious land, a land flowing with milk and honey – the home of the Canaanites, Hittites, Amorites, Perizzites, Hivites and Jebusites. And now the cry of the Israelites has reached me, and I have seen the way the Egyptians are oppressing them. So now go. I am sending you to Pharaoh to bring my people the Israelites out of Egypt."

But Moses said to God, "Who am I that I should go to Pharaoh and bring the Israelites out of Egypt?"

And God said, "I will be with you. And this will be the sign to you that it is I who have sent you: When you have brought the people out of Egypt, you will worship God on this mountain."

Moses said to God, "Suppose I go to the Israelites and say to them, 'The God of your fathers has sent me to you,' and they ask me, 'What is his name?' Then what shall I tell them?"

God said to Moses, "I AM WHO I AM. This is what you are to say to the Israelites: 'I AM has sent me to you.'"

Exodus 3:1-14

Rhema Word:

God's people are in bondage to the spirits of suicide and depression, and He desires to call them out. He sees your depression, senses your rejection, and hears your cries.

Many of you have tried to fight your battle against suicide and depression on your own and in the natural. God wants to show you that the battle against suicide and depression is a supernatural one that He desires to fight with and for you.

God needs your story, your testimony of healing and deliverance, to bring the next person out of their bondage. When you are asked where your help comes from, and when others ask who brought you from your bondage, you will say that the I AM WHO I AM sent you. The God of yesterday, today, and forevermore is bringing you out so He can use you to deliver others.

When He heals and delivers you, He will use you to help others, and you will worship Him for what He has done in your life. God has done it for me and given me this encounter with you. I have faith that God can and will heal you, too. All He needs is your "Here I am, God."

Who this Book is for:

The spirit of death hovered over me from a very young age. I know now that God intended many great things for my life. Had I allowed the spirit of death to win, I would not be where I am today – whole, free, and restored because of Jesus Christ.

This book is for you. It is both for people who know Jesus, and for those who don't. It's for people who have exhausted every other option to survive. It's for people who have made suicide attempts, and for those who are considering suicide but remain silent. This is for people who are openly suicidal and for those who externally express joy but are internally struggling. Many of you may have tried other natural solutions. I, too, turned to many things for help – alcohol, food, pills, and other addictions. Some things you've sought may not have been bad, like counseling, family, and friends, but you still walked away from these avenues feeling empty.

I'm here to share a different way to fight and win this battle. The world has been taught that the only way to overcome suicide is through natural solutions, like counseling or community groups. While these solutions should serve as supplements to your healing, they alone will not lead you to a breakthrough. I'm challenging you to consider suicide beyond the natural realm, and to consider it in the spiritual. The only path to true freedom from the spirit of suicide is through Jesus Christ.

Some may have encountered people who have claimed to be Christians, yet have ended up hurting you. Some of these people may have spoken to you about Jesus without reflecting His heart, thus turning you away from the most powerful resource in the universe. I'm sorry that these individuals were not accurate reflections of Jesus. Not everyone who claims His name is genuinely operating from His Spirit. We must know His word to discern who is truly following Him. I'm asking you to open your heart to try again, this time solely focusing on having a personal encounter with Jesus.

Some may be Christians who are frustrated at the fact that they are struggling with suicidal ideations and depression, even though they are also filled with the Holy Spirit. I ask that this population posture their hearts to seek the grace and love of God. You may be surrounded by individuals who challenge your faith because of your battle in this area. I challenge that it is through our weakness that Christ will show Himself strong in our lives (2 Corinthians 12:9).

This book will explain what the spirit of suicide is, what its roots are, and why some people are exposed to it more than others. We will explore the combination of external and personal factors that may have collectively contributed to your current state. The goal of this book is that you ultimately learn how to break the spirits of suicide and depression once and for all through Jesus Christ.

At various points in my life, I was every type of person who I am challenging to read this book. I was the preacher's daughter who grew up in church but had to learn how to choose God for myself in a world that was bombarding me with sin. I was the young girl who looked perfect outwardly but who chose to engage in sin to the point where my shame, guilt, silence, and sin overtook me and led to severe hopelessness internally. I was hurt by people claiming to be Christians while still trying to navigate my relationship with Jesus. I eventually recommitted to Christ, only to still be faced with the looming threat of suicide. Through it all, God healed and delivered me. My own testimony in this area led to many discoveries about the spirit of suicide that I now share with you. It may not feel like it now, but healing is possible for you, too.

My Testimony

Between the ages of 16 and 25, I experienced four major bouts of depression, anxiety, and suicidal ideations, or thoughts. When one looks at my life, one may not understand how I could struggle with suicidal thoughts – I was raised in a two-parent household, never lived in poverty, and had success from a very young age. I studied classical ballet for 16 years, was my class valedictorian in high school, won multiple state championship titles in track and field, and graduated from a prestigious college and Division I track program as the fastest woman in Service Academy history. Yet these successes became my identity, and they couldn't protect me from the emptiness that crept inside. I severely struggled with perfection, and this transpired into a burdensome load of anxiety. I felt isolated and lonely within my friendships due to my many obligations. I didn't feel I could speak with anyone because it didn't seem anyone around me could understand my perspective. My loneliness, emptiness, and severe anxiety amid my success, coupled with many other life experiences, opened the door for the spirit of death to hover over me for almost 10 years.

My first experience with depression occurred in high school, and I completely brushed it off. I attended a military high school, not because I was a bad kid, but because it was one of the better schools in my community. I'm the youngest of four siblings, separated in age by at least 11 years from each of them. Thus, my siblings and I had estranged connections until I was older. Moreover, my parents worked demanding jobs that kept us from spending significant time together. Most of my peers knew me as a "goody-two-shoes" because of my family's values and involvement in the church. Many saw my success and were envious or harsh toward me, as they were tired of seeing me constantly at the top. I could never tell as a teenager who was truly on my side, as my success isolated me from many of my same-aged peers. This intense isolation from my peers, my siblings, and my parents was the devil's foothold to plant depressive thoughts in my ears. At 16, I was unsure of what I was dealing with, and I didn't share my experiences with my parents because I didn't want them to worry. Moreover, I knew that my family had established a culture of excellence that I didn't want to intrude upon. I grew up in a Black family in the South, with parents and grandparents who intentionally pursued higher education and prestigious opportunities that were not open to the generations prior. I am incredibly grateful for the opportunities that were afforded to me, and I also must acknowledge that the pressure and perfection of Black excellence also contributed to my deteriorating mental health, especially since I was not receiving or seeking developmental assistance in navigating this area of my life.

      My second experience occurred during my first year at The United States Military Academy, and it coincided with my first step toward a suicide attempt. The United States Military Academy, commonly known as West Point, is a leadership institution that produces many of the Army's next officers and leaders. At West Point, cadets must live by the honor code: "A cadet will not lie, cheat, steal, nor tolerate those who do." My freshman roommate was sleeping with a senior. Other upperclassmen who were aware of the circumstances encouraged me to speak up, yet they didn't say a word. While this may not be a significant issue at other colleges, it was against the rules at West Point due to the numerous leadership roles that seniors hold compared to the vulnerability that first-year students face under their leadership. First-year students are required to follow the rules issued by seniors. Of course, a senior sleeping with a freshman may give that individual an unfair advantage and/or put them in a vulnerable position to be abused. I decided to say something to the company leadership, and many of the people who encouraged me to speak were the same people who turned against me after I spoke up. This circumstance led to a severe rejection, which in turn prompted me to question my worth in the world. My roommate caught me sitting on the windowsill of our barracks room, pondering the jump. At that moment, I remember considering that this one jump could end this tormenting sense of rejection and hurt. However, having been caught at the window, my team leader took me to a counseling session the next day. I smiled just enough during the session to convince the counselor that this was a one-off situation that wouldn't happen again. She never processed the paperwork for my session.

I also expressed suicidal thoughts at my first duty station in the Army, which lasted over two years. I didn't seek help, and I didn't honestly believe I had time to do so. My unit was engaged in multiple, world-impacting missions, including the removal of troops from Afghanistan and stability operations in Eastern Europe due to the conflict between Russia and Ukraine. As a young leader, I was expected to be present as much as possible, and as a perfectionist, I strived to make that happen.

My daily schedule typically involved a 4:30 am wake-up, and I wouldn't leave the office until around 8 or 9 pm, even when we weren't planning missions. After a year of this cycle, I acquired a new, unrealistically demanding, and highly critical commander who was eventually quietly fired for his toxicity toward me, the soldiers, and the unit. He was the type of leader who placed additional and unrealistic requirements upon the unit in the middle of high-tempo and already stressful mission sequences, pushing an already exhausted force beyond an acceptable level of risk. When missions failed or severe mistakes were made, he would often pass the responsibility for his faulty leadership decisions onto his subordinate leaders, resulting in the firing of two junior leaders under his command. In my experience with him, I saw him as a cunning serpent. He knew just the right words to say to others outside of our organization to keep them from knowing his true nature. Yet, internally, he would speak to me with an exhaustingly belligerent and critical tongue that brought back the same spirit of rejection and mental torment that moved me to question my worth. After an altercation in the field with this commander, I once again found myself thinking of a way to quickly end the agony of the recurring theme of opposition, isolation, and defeat that I felt from his words and actions. After much contemplation, I asked my friend to keep the bottle of pills from my hygiene bag that I was considering swallowing. My friend took the pills and made me promise to seek counseling the next day. I attended the counseling session, but I only had two more sessions before moving to an entirely new duty station.

My fourth and final bout with suicide occurred at my second duty station. I mistakenly believed that I was free from the spirit of suicide because I changed locations and left my previous boss and all other opposing critics behind. To be clear, changing environments is necessary and is always crucial in toxic situations, but unless an evil spirit is broken in the spiritual realm, it may continue to plague you regardless of where you go. Thus, even after I changed duty stations, the spirit of suicide crept in again. The trigger this time was the narcissistic tendencies of the man I had formed a romantic relationship with; his words and actions led to my feelings of inadequacy. The same thoughts of rejection and abandonment from my experiences at 16 were revealed in this experience at 25. After months of trying to satisfy him without receiving any hope or promise from him that the relationship could go anywhere, I eventually reached a breaking point of hopelessness, as my spirit could no longer contain what I kept trying to cover up, hide, and move on from. The same man I blamed for my inadequacy delivered me to the hospital for expressing a desire to commit suicide.

After years of silently navigating this issue, I had no choice but to expose everything to the light. The Army notifies one's family and chain of command during serious hospitalizations; thus, the silence about this topic was broken, and my family finally became aware of the evil spirit that was plaguing me for almost 10 years.

Surprisingly, the hospital room was the place where my heart began to heal.

Sitting in my hospital bed, I clearly heard God's voice say, "Are you listening to me now?" He was reminding me that He had been trying to get my attention for some time, but like Adam and Eve after committing their sin, I was trying to hide my reality from my family, myself, and God. Over the course of ten years, I racked up a rap sheet of sin, shame, guilt, pain, trauma, rejection, and abandonment to the point where I was ready to die. But this isn't God's intention for His creation. I didn't know it then, but I know now that God used that hospital room as the beginning of my restoration and healing. He put me in a position to make an obvious and straightforward decision: give up and die, or give it to Him and live. At this point, I realized how much power I had given my emotions, other people, and my own negative thoughts to dictate my life sentence. Being chained to my hospital bed with nowhere else to go, I decided it was time I chose to give it to God instead.

I initially committed my life to Jesus Christ at nine years old in my family's church in Milledgeville, Georgia. I remember being in a church service where my father, the pastor, called everyone who wanted to be saved by Jesus to come to the altar. I heard God prompting me, at nine, to meet Him at that altar, so I obeyed. In that moment, I confessed my sins, declared Jesus as my Lord and Savior, and dedicated my life to Christ. Still, it was in that hospital bed, at 25 years old, that that same Voice I had neglected in high school and college spoke to me. I listened and recommitted my life to Him. I had no choice; He was my only place of survival and the last string I held onto. Being in the hospital forced me to look back over my journey and see that my experiences with depression, anxiety, and suicidal ideations were so beyond the natural world. This was a spiritual battle that I didn't have the knowledge to fight. I was trying to blame the man I was romantically involved with, the toxic boss, and everyone else in my life who ever held a part in hurting me. Don't get me wrong, I know God's justice will prevail over them if they do not repent! But I know now that I gave them too much power over my life. I tried to take God's justice into my own hands and serve it to them by taking myself out of the fight, but it was never my job to serve as God's justice system. Most detrimentally, I placed their importance in my life over God's. Think about it: I cared more about what these people did to me, said about me, or potentially thought about me than about what *God* had done, said, or thought about me. God's word says that we are beautifully and wonderfully made (Psalm 139:14). God's word says that we are heirs to the Kingdom of Heaven (Romans 8:17). God's word says that His plans are that He would prosper us and not harm us (Jeremiah 29:11). So why was I listening to these crazy people and allowing them to almost kill me? I placed more value on them than on God. In other words, I had made them my idols.

Many of us underestimate what an idol is; we tend to make the incorrect assumption that idols are only little statues that people bow down to. An idol is anything that we place above God. The first two of the Ten Commandments state that we shall have no other (little "g") gods above the one true God, and that we shall not make any idols (Exodus 20:2-17). My heart was driven to please and serve others from a well of hurt and manipulation, stemming from my own wounds. I was focused on being the perfect preacher's daughter, academic, and track athlete. I hoped that my success in these areas would satisfy my spirit and justify my worth in living. I wouldn't give the Creator of the universe ten minutes of prayer time or Bible reading time, which has been clinically proven to reduce depression and anxiety (Macinnis). Instead, I gave my idols, who drained the life out of me, hours of my time and mental energy. But *that's* the issue! Anything else we use besides God to justify our worth or existence is an idol because we're centering that thing above Him. Moreover, these idols will ALWAYS disappoint us because these things – success, fame, money, and position – while they bring temporary satisfaction, can never tame your hungry soul. Our souls long for perfect love, significance, and connection, and the only source that ultimately satisfies, heals, and always affirms our worth is Jesus Christ.

You did not deserve the terrible things that happened to you. As mentioned earlier, God's justice will prevail in the physical realm, the spiritual realm, or both. But no one can force someone to apologize for any hurt they have caused. It is now your responsibility to heal, not only survive, but to truly live in accordance with your God-ordained purpose. Sitting in the hospital bed and having no choice but to hold on to Christ for survival brought me to a place of understanding that while my experiences hurt me, my idolatry and sin also contributed to the open door that allowed the spirit of suicide to run rampant in my life. I had to take ownership and responsibility for *that* side of myself, too. Moreover, I spent too much time only trying to fight suicide naturally, in the physical realm. I called the national suicide hotline, attended non-Christian counseling, attempted to connect with friends, and spent money on self-care trips. The woman on the other end of the line for the suicide hotline was going to allow me to leave the phone call without a suicide prevention action plan. The non-Christian counseling eventually felt empty because the counselor's worldly suggestions weren't rooted in biblical truth. My "friends" couldn't relate to my experiences, and God eventually exposed that many of these "friends" were keeping me in bondage to sin and distancing me from Him. While the self-care trips were a great escape, I always returned to my empty reality. The only one who filled my heart, healed my soul, and made me whole was Jesus Christ.

    I want to be clear; I am not saying that these natural solutions are not helpful, and I am by no means suggesting that people shouldn't utilize the national suicide hotline. Utilize all these resources because they can provide temporary relief. They are the bandages for the wound but are not the solution for your wholeness and healing. They should be considered in conjunction with Christ, as a supplement to the fullness that His presence and healing provide.

    As I reflect on my journey, I am grateful that God kept me so that I could share my story and lessons learned with you. Romans 8:28 says that "in all things God works for the good of those who love him, who have been called according to his purpose." Your experience is no exception. I found myself fighting suicide for almost ten years, and its recurrence brought me to the reality that the fight against it is spiritual. Thus, we must understand how the spiritual world operates in order to fight properly.

HOW THE SPIRITUAL WORLD OPERATES

"For our struggle is not against flesh and blood, but against rulers, against the authorities, against the powers of this dark world and against the spiritual forces of evil in the heavenly realms."

Ephesians 6:12

How the Spiritual World Operates

Explaining the depth of how the spiritual world operates would overtake this book to the point where the topic of suicide would get lost in rabbit trails of information. Thus, this section will condense how the spiritual world operates through two universal truths: God's love for us, and Satan's war against God's love.

In all honesty, our humanness prevents us from understanding the totality of how God operates because His ways are not like our ways (Isaiah 55:8-9). Thus, no amount of theology or study will ever bring us to understand the vastness of God and all the ways He's decided to move. Arguably, the more we dive into theological rabbit trails, the more we escape the simple yet profound revelations that the Lord desires to bring us to through His word.

Please understand that I am not discounting study time; dwelling with God's scriptures and gaining understanding with additional God-breathed resources is essential. I only propose that the case of suicide requires us to focus on the heart of God more than any religious or ritualistic obligation to understand the fullness of theological concepts. So, this section intentionally provides a brief overview of the spiritual world so that you may have an understanding as to why the devil is after many people as it pertains to suicide.

Universal Truth 1

I want to start with one central, universal truth: God is a loving God who desires a relationship with you. Many may struggle to believe this truth. God sent His son, Jesus Christ, who was fully God and fully man, as a living sacrifice for our sins. Jesus died via crucifixion – one of the most treacherous ways a person could die. Moreover, He died when He didn't deserve it. He was blameless and without sin, yet bore the full weight of it so that we no longer live under sin's yoke. After He died, He resurrected on the third day, proving that He defeated death, hell, and the grave, and He took His rightful place next to His Father in heaven. During the time of the Old Testament, also known as the Old Covenant, or the time before the sacrifice of Jesus Christ, God's people would constantly have to provide various sacrifices to atone for their sins. God saw that we, as His creation, were imperfect and were bound to break His laws; we needed a perfect sacrifice to cover us from all past, present, and future sins. Thus, God submitted His holiness to become flesh through Jesus Christ so that the weight of sin would no longer be our responsibility or burden. Under the New Testament, or the New

Covenant, which is the time after the sacrifice and resurrection of Jesus Christ, when believers of Jesus Christ sin, they have access to the gifts of repentance and grace, rather than religious sacrifices. This means that when we make mistakes, instead of carrying the burden of that mistake, we can confess our sins to Jesus, turn from our wrong actions or thoughts, and receive God's forgiveness. God loves us so much that when we repent for our mistakes, He offers his forgiveness freely. No other being can do that entirely, except that Jesus Christ transforms him.

Universal Truth 2

The conversation about God's love tends to spark a fair question: If God is so loving, why does He allow evil to exist? Couldn't He eradicate it? Why is He allowing you to experience this battle? This leads to the following universal truth – a spiritual war is being waged between God's Kingdom of light and love, and Satan's kingdom of darkness and death, and that spiritual war spills over into the physical realm. Parents abuse their children; manipulative businesses take advantage of the poor; the list of encounters and toxic cycles that cause tremendous hurt, shame, and guilt continues, and so often there seems to be no way of healing from the trauma they cause. This war between good and evil, coupled with the hurt we carry from life's blows, encourages us to walk independently of God and make our own choices, which often leads to disaster. There is another way.

God always intended for us to walk with Him as His children. He knew and formed each of us before we were even a thought to our parents (Psalm 139:13). He predestined a plan for each of our lives (Jeremiah 29:11). He is so patient and loving that He wants none of us to perish (2 Peter 3:9). We must recognize that Satan is angry because he and his crew of angels were kicked out of heaven for their pride and rebellion against God (Revelation 12:1-12). Thus, Satan does everything in his power to fight against everything that God made good and perfect. He intentionally uses people to hurt us to turn us away from the one source that can save and heal us.

All of us are either vessels for light, or for darkness. When someone who hurts and does evil things toward us, they are acting as a vessel, or representative, of Satan's kingdom. This is rebellion against God. When we choose to live lifestyles of sin against God, we choose to serve as vessels of darkness instead of light. Contrarily, when we act in accordance with the traits of Jesus, with the fruits of the Spirit, and the Word of God, we choose to be vessels for God's kingdom. The key is that God has given humans a choice, and free will. God is a just, righteous, and covenant-honoring God. Being just, righteous, and covenant-honoring means that God is always lawfully right in conduct and character, and does not act contrary to His Word. God allowed all of us to have free will. God desires people who will choose to be with Him. None are forced to serve him. He established our wills so that we would be free to decide whom we will serve. God is so gracious that He created humans in His image and established us to have dominion over the earth (Genesis 1:26-28). His original intention was for us to partner with Him to accomplish His will over the earth. The key here is that God gave humans free will to *choose* to partner with Him. He never wanted to be a dictator who forced us to follow Him; He desired that we would choose to partner with Him.

  However, because we have free will, many humans choose to live against God, which opens the door for them to be used as vessels to harm others. Thus, evil is allowed to prevail, not because God desires it, but because humans have used their free will to perpetrate evil. And because God is a covenant-honoring God, He will not go against His promises to give humans that free will. We are responsible for how we will use our dominion on this earth, and many have chosen to use it for Satan's kingdom by doing so much harm to others. John 10:10 states that "Satan comes to steal, kill, and destroy, but Jesus came to offer life, and life more abundantly." Satan's purpose is to harm you, but God's purpose is to prosper you *with* Him. In Satan's attempts to destroy you, he tries to convince you that everything happening to you is God's fault so that he can keep you away from God's Kingdom of light. He knows that if you become free from suicide and depression, you will be a threat to him. Thus, Satan uses your experiences and the people closest to you to contribute to your harm. However, God is so great that He can use every terrible thing that Satan tries to use to knock you out to instead transform and elevate you – "You prepare a table before me in the presence of my enemies. You anoint my head with oil; my cup overflows" (Psalm 23:5).

WHAT IS THE SPIRIT OF SUICIDE?

When Jesus got out of the boat, a man with an impure spirit came from the tombs to meet him.

This man lived in the tombs, and no one could bind him anymore, not even with a chain. For he had often been chained hand and foot, but he tore the chains apart and broke the irons on his feet. No one was strong enough to subdue him.

Night and day among the tombs and in the hills he would cry out and cut himself with stones.

When he saw Jesus from a distance, he ran and fell on his knees in front of him. He shouted at the top of his voice, "What do you want with me, Jesus, Son of the Most High God? In God's name don't torture me!" For Jesus had said to him, "Come out of this man, you impure spirit!"

Then Jesus asked him, "What is your name?" "My name is Legion," [the impure spirit] replied, "for we are many."

And he begged Jesus again and again not to send them out of the area.

A large herd of pigs was feeding on the nearby hillside. The demons begged Jesus, "Send us among the pigs; allow us to go into them." He gave them permission, and the impure spirits came out and went into the pigs. The herd, about two thousand in number, rushed down the steep bank into the lake and were drowned.

Those tending the pigs ran off and reported this in the town and countryside, and the people went out to see what had happened. When they came to Jesus, they saw the man who had been possessed by the legion of demons sitting there, dressed and in his right mind; and they were afraid. Those who had seen it told the people what had happened to the demon-possessed man – and told about the pigs as well.

Mark 5:2-16

Rhema Word:

When the spirit of suicide came against you, it did not come alone; it carried its brothers with it to occupy your heart and mind.

The spirit of suicide is the rotten fruit on the tree, but it has many roots that work together to take you out. Many of you may not see yourselves as demon-possessed or oppressed. Many argue theologically about whether believers of Jesus can be possessed. Regardless of the technical terms, those who know Jesus and those who don't are in bondage to suicidal ideations. God simply wants you free.

Let my testimony be evidence to you: I was so caught in my anxiety, shame, guilt, silence, and sin; I was hearing voices in my head and couldn't sleep at night; I believed all the things I was experiencing were simply natural diagnoses. God exposed that a legion of evil spirits was attacking me; I believed that listening to the thoughts (or demonic voices) to kill myself was the only way to achieve peace. These thoughts never came from God.

Many of you have been experiencing similar attacks for years. You have been full of rage, sadness, bitterness, rejection, and a lack of peace that is driving you mentally mad, just so that you believe that the only relief will be in ending it all. You have been searching for peace in everything else, and God wants to bring you out and give you rest.

By His hand, He can call out evil spirits with simple words; they know Jesus Christ by name and have no choice but to obey His word and authority.

You *will* walk, live, and thrive in peace by the name, the blood, and the authority of Jesus Christ.

The Spirit of Suicide

Any spirit that is not of the Holy Spirit is an evil spirit. The Holy Spirit is also known as the Advocate, or Spirit of Truth, and was sent to us from the Father after Jesus' resurrection to testify about Jesus Christ (John 15:26). Thus, any spirit that is not the Holy Spirit carries a lying spirit that was sent to you to testify against the work of Jesus. Evil spirits are, many times, synonymously referred to as demons. To be clear, the Bible specifies that there are levels of evil powers (Ephesians 6:12), but throughout this book, I will continue referring to suicide as an evil spirit or demon. These demons are the same fallen angels that Lucifer took with him when he fell from heaven; thus, they are Satan's minions that go out to do his dirty work.

God is omniscient and omnipresent, meaning He is all-knowing and present everywhere simultaneously. Satan doesn't carry these qualities, and he instead operates by first introducing a singular, taunting thought that is against God. After this thought is planted, Satan will leave you alone because he knows that most of the time, humans will allow that thought to grow until it's all-consuming. Many tend to allow the thoughts that pop into their heads to carry negative perspectives that cause them to go down rabbit holes until their thought patterns produce anxiety and depression. If most of our thoughts lead us spiraling down a negative, anxious, or depressive rabbit hole, we have just allowed our brains to do Satan's job for him! After we carry these thought patterns for years, we begin attaching them to our identity, which God never intended for us to do. We may express statements like, "I'm just an angry or sad person" – without understanding that we're attaching the spirits associated with these emotions to ourselves and our bloodlines! God never intended for us to let our emotions define our identities.

The spirit of suicide operates in the exact same way. It creeps in with a singular, Satan-planted thought, and before long, our minds will dwell on that thought without submitting it to God. Weeks, months, and years of suicidal thoughts begin to manifest deep-rooted thought patterns, lifestyle choices, and actions that lead us closer and closer to a real death.

As an example, consider one of God's prophets, Elijah. Elijah was a strong man of faith. In 1Kings 18:16-40, on behalf of God, Elijah confronts King Ahab for Israel's sinful idolatry. Elijah is also famous for challenging 850 false prophets who believed their false gods were real. During this encounter, Elijah trusted God so much that he challenged the false prophets to call on their god to rain fire from heaven, but their god could not follow through. Elijah called on the one true God, and He rained fire from heaven for all to witness!

In the very next chapter, however, this same mighty prophet of God allows the thought of fear to creep in as King Ahab's wife, Jezebel, threatens to kill him. Even though he just witnessed God's miracle and supernatural covering, his fear of Jezebel manifested to the point where he wanted to run away from his calling as a prophet. His deep depression made him pray for death! I want to be clear that Elijah's issue wasn't the fact that the thought of fear came; all humans experience this emotion at some point in life. The issue lies in his allowance of the emotion to completely overtake him to the point that he desired death. He, like many, allowed the emotion to almost snatch his identity and destiny away.

God's gentle whisper eventually reminds Elijah of his purpose and the importance of continuing. By God's grace, I believe He can remind you of who you are, too. Typically, when we associate an emotion with our identity, we, like Elijah, have challenging experiences or considerations in our minds that may contribute to our mental state. Elijah had a mountaintop experience by proving that hundreds of prophets were wrong... but he was still the only true prophet in all of Israel who was faithful to God; I can only imagine how lonely he must have felt standing for God in a world that was totally against Him. Like Elijah, you may also feel isolated and believe that you're going through things that others around you can't seem to comprehend.

I encourage you that, just as God whispered to Elijah, He can whisper to you, too. He can inform and remind you of your purpose. The spirit of death tries to knock out God's greatest warriors before their time; that's why it's after you. There's something amazing you're meant to do for God's kingdom that the enemy knows is a threat to the kingdom of darkness. Consider the spirits that operated in Pharaoh and King Herod. In the book of Exodus, Pharaoh decrees that all newborn Hebrew boys must be killed by throwing them in the Nile River. Pharaoh feared that the Israelites would become numerous enough to take over the land of Egypt. Satan knew that a deliverer was going to be born, so he tried to use Pharaoh to kill God's children and shatter God's plan – except Moses was born, and with God, he delivered God's people from 400 years of Egyptian slavery. Similarly, in the book of Matthew, King Herod issues a decree to kill all male infants under two years old. Herod received news that the Israelites' Messiah would be born. Again, the devil knew that he could use King Herod to kill an entire generation of young boys in an attempt to destroy God's chosen Messiah... except that Jesus was born, and He fulfilled His purpose as the Messiah and conquered sin once and for all. Let this be your encouragement –

the fact that the spirit of death has tried coming after you is proof that there's something untapped and unleashed on the inside of you that God needs for His kingdom!

The Fruit Reveals the Roots

Three major roots paved the way for the spirit of suicide to plague my life: shame and guilt, silence, and idolatry. This is not an exhaustive list, and there are many more roots associated with suicide. I'm focusing on these three because of their significance in my breakthrough, and I believe that your ability to uproot them will also lead to your breakthrough.

Consider evil spirits that have significant strongholds over your life like rotten trees. The head of the tree, where the leaves and fruit reside, represents the head spirit in charge that you may be attempting to fight. However, every evil spirit that is operating in your life and that you're having difficulty removing is deeply rooted with a collection of other spirits that are also operating in your life.

When picturing the spirit of suicide, imagine suicide as the rotten fruit or dead leaves at the head of the tree; you can tell suicide is producing fruit in your life based on your mindset, your speech, and your actions. At the base of the suicide tree, there's a root system that houses the spirits of shame and guilt, silence, idolatry, and others. Roots feed from the environment they are in. If we surround ourselves with people who are contributing to our shame and guilt, who display that operating in silence is okay, or are also walking in idolatry, the roots of these spirits grow deeper to nourish more rotten, suicidal fruit. Thus, it's essential to address the spirit of suicide at its roots and to remove ourselves from environments that produce evil fruit.

I, like many of you, was fighting suicide for an extensive amount of time, and I could always feel it when it was creeping back up. My problem was that I was trying to fight suicide in isolation without addressing its roots. Time after time, I would pray against or rebuke the spirit of suicide, completely unaware that the spirit would return, bringing more of its demon friends with it. Jesus states, "When an impure spirit comes out of a person, it goes through arid places seeking rest and does not find it. Then it says, 'I will return to the house I left.' When it arrives, it finds the house unoccupied, swept clean and put in order. Then it goes and takes with it seven other spirits more wicked than itself, and they go and live there. And the final condition of that person is worse than the first" (Matthew 12:43-45).

If you find that you have been fighting suicide, but it continues to return, it's more than likely brought back other spirits that are causing havoc in your life. You must address the spirit of suicide AND its roots, or it will continue to plague you. I must address the reality that because the devil's mission is to "steal, kill, and destroy," he will always attempt to oppress you (John 10:10). The point I am making is that when you finally defeat these spirits with Jesus Christ, even when the enemy comes to attack, you will have a new way of fighting that won't give the enemy the right to enter your dwelling anymore.

Shame and Guilt

Shame and guilt can keep you trapped in a cycle of condemnation that keeps you stuck in suicidal ideations and depression. God never intended this for you. Shame and guilt involve negative evaluations of oneself, but their focus and effects differ.

Shame focuses on the self; experiencing this emotion causes us to feel as though our entire being is terrible. This leads to a desire to hide, disappear, or escape a situation, much like Adam and Eve in the Garden of Eden, who tried to hide from God after they first sinned (Genesis 3:8).

Guilt centers our behavior; we experience guilt when we regret a specific action or behavior. Guilt can lead us to change our behavior, but it can also lock us into negative thought patterns about that behavior, causing us to become ashamed of ourselves.

Condemnation is the act of rendering a guilty verdict. We typically self-condemn or are condemned by others when we should be applying God's grace. Condemnation makes us believe that we will always be judged without the hope of forgiveness. But Romans 8:1-2 says that "there is now no condemnation for those who are in Christ Jesus" because Jesus "has set you free from the law of sin and death." Moreover, 2 Corinthians 5:17 states, "If anyone is in Christ, the new creation has come: the old has gone, the new is here!" Yet, operating from shame and guilt keeps us in bondage to an old mindset of condemnation, even though we have been given the ability to operate from our newness in God's freedom.

To clarify, those who serve Jesus Christ are promised that they don't have to live in condemnation. Many people, however, are still plagued by condemnation because they feel no hope of being forgiven or are plagued by the sins others committed against them; thus, the doors to shame and guilt remain open in their hearts.

God desires that we walk knowing that we are no longer in bondage to suicide and depression; we are free to walk in His authority and power because we carry His name. The law of condemnation desires that you punish or sentence yourself to mental or physical torment because you disapprove of something you have done or experienced. Operating from shame, guilt, and condemnation makes us judge ourselves before allowing God to, yet God tends to be more merciful toward us than we are toward ourselves. If you look at the Israelites, even when God was upset with them and allowed them to experience a consequence for their actions, He still acknowledged them as His children. He could have judged them according to the full weight of the law, but He constantly showed mercy.

Mercy reflects God's compassion toward us; it's when God chooses to withhold judgment. In God's mercy, He gives us the opportunity to make different decisions. You must choose to rest the burden of all shame and guilt on Jesus' shoulders, so it no longer has a hold over you.

Pray against shame and guilt as you fight the spirit of suicide. Tear down old thought patterns of condemnation and ask God to transform your mind. You may be allowing shame and guilt to constantly condemn you to the point of suicide. You may be surrounded by so-called "friends" and unhealthy family members who condemn you for every mistake. You may be holding on to things that you did or that others did to you months or years ago because you are placing these mistakes on yourself and not in Jesus' hands. You feel the weight of sins that He already paid for. There is another way to live – "Come to me, all you who are weary and burdened, and I will give you rest. Take my yoke upon you and learn from me, for I am gentle and humble in heart, and you will find rest for your souls. For my yoke is easy and my burden is light" (Matthew 11:28-30).

Silence

Silence, not speaking up in dangerous situations, and not discussing your feelings and internal thoughts, ensures that suicide's bond over your life grips you generationally. Families who practice silence tend to be plagued by severe circumstances that are only revealed after the damage has been done, all because no one took the time to share their experiences and lessons learned with the next generation. Some have tried expressing their painful experiences, only to have their family and friends discount their words due to the fear of what exposing these secrets might mean. I challenge you to ask questions and host the conversations that no one else seems willing or able to have. You may experience nervousness, and some family members may deny you the opportunity to connect; ask God to grant you the boldness to speak. Trust that breaking the silence about your issues will lead to healing and breakthrough; God will meet your heart. Psalm 51:17 states, "My sacrifice, O God, is a broken spirit; a broken and contrite heart you, God, will not despise."

    Silence opens the door for the enemy to establish generational curses in your bloodline. My firsthand experience with silence taught me how to take an honest look at my family, and I encourage you to do the same with yours. Compare any patterns you have noticed running rampant in your own life and the lives of your relatives with the last three mothers and the last three fathers on both sides of your family. You will notice evidence of the generational curses and blessings that exist within your bloodline.

    Generational blessings result from the topics within a bloodline that were addressed and acted upon. This may look like someone in your family recognizing how generational abuse, alcoholism, or trauma negatively impacts the family. Instead of following unhealthy patterns in the family, they choose to seek the Lord, counsel, and community to heal and to do things differently. The family curse breakers set an example for the next generation, showing that the family is capable of breaking unhealthy cycles. Once a cycle is broken, the space that was previously filled with trauma and abuse is now able to be filled with blessings like healthy relationships, healthy families, and pure love.

    Generational curses result from hidden and silenced issues. Take the same person from the previous example and imagine that instead of recognizing *and* addressing unhealthy cycles, they participate in and perpetuate them. The generational curse enhancer in the family is someone who may or may not recognize the unhealthy patterns that have been passed down to them. The person who is unable to recognize unhealthy patterns in their family is likely to pass these patterns on to the next generation due to a lack of awareness. It's like, say, grandpa's father was an abusive alcoholic, and his children were also abusive alcoholics. This might continue for generations. Scripture says that God's people perish because we lack knowledge (Hosea 4:6). Thus, generations of families have been plagued by depression and suicide simply because they lack an awareness of what is hurting those they love. The person who recognizes generational issues but fails to address them due to silence will also pass on unhealthy patterns to the next generation. This person may be able to identify an issue. Still, their inability to address the problem by teaching the next generation how to overcome it will be the open door Satan uses to perpetuate that unhealthy pattern in the next generation. Both blessings and curses are passed on to the next generation, and both carry fruit. It is up to the members within a bloodline to choose how they will utilize their free will in their lifetime, but trust that their choices also impact you. When we fail to address our sins, bondage, or issues, we will pass them on to our children to solve – or continue!

Silence goes hand in hand with shame and guilt. When our hearts cry out that we are ashamed of who we are or what we've done, we adopt the incorrect mindset that we are protecting our families by not sharing those experiences. Yet, instead of protecting our families, silence actually sets our families up to take ownership of the issues that God meant for us to address in our lifetimes. Do yourself and your bloodline a favor and break the hold that silence has had over you and your family.

Consider Abram's example (also known as Abraham) in Genesis 12 and 20. Within both chapters, Abraham moves to different locations and lies about his wife Sarai (also known as Sarah) by claiming her as his sister. He lies to Pharaoh (Genesis 12) and Abimelech (Genesis 20) because his wife is so beautiful that he fears the leaders will kill him to get access to her. Years later, in Genesis 26, Abraham's son, Isaac, makes the *same mistake* his father had in Genesis 20. Like his father, Isaac also had a beautiful wife, Rebekah. Isaac expressed the same lie as his father to the king of his time by claiming Rebekah as his sister. Abraham and Isaac's actions harmed their wives and almost brought spiritual consequences upon the kings involved. These passages display Abraham's lying pattern, which manifested in his son expressing the exact same lie. Moreover, Isaac's son, Jacob, perpetuated this lying spirit as he lied and stole his brother's birthright (Genesis 27:36). Thus, biblically, we see that generational patterns exist and how unhealthy patterns can be passed down across generations when we fail to address the issues. I wonder if Abraham's bloodline would have been plagued by lying had Abraham simply shared his mistake and learned lesson with his son.

When we open our mouths and speak about our struggles, we place ourselves in a position to:

1. Receive help.
2. Break the yoke of someone else's bondage, who may be experiencing similar struggles.
3. Close every open door that silence has ever used to wreak havoc over us and our bloodlines.

Many issues like rape, adultery, broken marriages, and especially suicide are allowed to plague our families because of silence. It must stop with you. I was the one responsible for breaking many things in my family. I began asking my parents difficult questions. At first, these encounters were awkward, but God met our hearts with so much restoration, which continues today. My mother admitted to me about her bouts with suicide, depression, and antidepressants, and she revealed her ability to see suicidal tendencies in her mother, too. Having this information clarified my fight against suicide because it allowed me to go to God with direct prayer strategies.

I also understand that many may not have the luxury of communicating with members of their family due to death. I want to be clear that now is not the time to seek opportunities to connect with the dead, as this is known as necromancy and is a form of witchcraft. The Bible is clear that the dead can no longer speak (Job 7:9-10); thus, any attempt to communicate with the dead invites evil spirits into your life who pose as your ancestors. I understand that many may be frustrated because they are experiencing horrible things and are hurt because they have no natural way of knowing what is in their bloodline. However, God can reveal things to you supernaturally! Ask God to reveal what you need to address within your bloodline.

When I didn't know what to ask or where to start because my grandparents were deceased, I sought God to reveal to me the information I would need to fight. He spoke to me through dreams, visions, and Strong's Concordance numbers. Open your heart expectantly, and He will reveal information to you.

"Ask and it will be given to you; seek and you will find; knock and the door will be opened to you. For everyone who asks receives; the one who seeks finds; and to the one who knocks, the door will be opened" (Matthew 7:7-8).

THE HARDEST PART

42

The spirit of the Sovereign Lord is on me, because the Lord has anointed me to proclaim good news to the poor. He has sent me to bind up the brokenhearted, to proclaim freedom for the captives and release from darkness for the prisoners, to proclaim the year of the Lord's favor and the day of vengeance of our God, to comfort all who mourn,

and provide for those who grieve in Zion – to bestow on them a crown of beauty instead of ashes, the oil of joy instead of mourning, and a garment of praise instead of a spirit of despair. They will be called oaks of righteousness, a planting of the Lord for the display of his splendor.

They will rebuild the ancient ruins and restore the places long devastated; they will renew the ruined cities that have been devastated for generations.

Isaiah 61:1-4.

Rhema Word:

The Lord desires your heart. He knows that darkness and despair are not your portion. He wants to restore you. It's time to surrender all darkness to Him.

Many people have placed their justifications as to why they should no longer be here at the center of their hearts, where God should be. Your decision to focus on these thought patterns stems from a profound need for God's love.

You have looked for love, approval, and acceptance in all the wrong places. And every place you looked for love only drew you closer to death.

God will take every dead thing inside and around you and revive it to life. Let every unhealthy thought pattern go, turn to Him, and find abundant life (John 10:10).

Idolatry

Idolatry is one of the sneakiest roots associated with suicide. It revolves around how our *own* choice to center unhealthy mindsets and coping mechanisms in our hearts above God contributes to cycles of ideations and depression. To be clear, I don't believe that most people knowingly pursue idolatry. Most of us have a genuine desire for soul-fulfilling things, such as love and connection, which should be fulfilled first by God and then by a healthy community. However, when we're hurting and desire immediate relief, it's easy to rely on temporarily fulfilling things instead of seeking God as our source. What is first in your mind and thoughts? I challenge each to consider how centering other things in your life instead of God may be paving the way for suicide to have access to you.

When we choose to be with Christ, we become part of His church; therefore, we are also His bride (Ephesians 5:21-27). So, you can view your relationship with Christ as if you are in a marriage, a significant relationship, or a deep friendship with Him. Imagine Christ as your spouse or best friend; just like you wouldn't want your spouse cheating on you, or your best friend hurting you, God is a jealous God, and He doesn't want to be cheated on or brokenhearted either. Thus, when we harbor an unhealthy mindset and prioritize going to anything besides Him as a coping mechanism for healing, we expose the idolatry of choosing everything else instead of Him. We expose that maybe we don't fully believe that God is who He says He is. God's heart is grieved in these circumstances, and we remain in bondage because we've chosen things that cannot heal us as a substitute for healing. God is the ultimate healer and desires you to drink living waters that never run dry from His well (John 4:13-14).

In one sense, many have used coping mechanisms to keep themselves from experiencing suicidal ideations. I argue that without Jesus, only using coping mechanisms to heal shifts one's bondage from one focus point to another… because as soon as the replaced coping mechanism fails, many find themselves scrambling for the next thing to fill their cup.

To explain, the Centers for Disease Control and Prevention (CDC) acknowledge individual risk factors like substance use, loss of financial or job status, a sense of hopelessness, and many others as reasons why people commit suicide or are on the brink of it (CDC). However, the CDC also offers personal factors like using family and friends as reasons for living or a "strong cultural identity" as ways to protect against suicide risk (CDC). As mentioned in a previous section, these solutions may be used as a temporary fix for an issue but cannot serve as one's *complete* source of healing and reason for living. What happens when the family member we're trying to rely on must move far away, or when the cultural identity isn't one we relate to? Many find themselves distraught and back in the same place of brokenness and hopelessness because they attempt to make something else the center of their heart, where God desires to be. And whatever our hearts center on above God is an idol.

Many have also placed deeply rooted and unhealthy reasons as to why they should harm themselves at the center of their hearts. People who experience suicidal ideations may be driven to these unhealthy thought patterns because of their circumstances, experiences, or the people around them. Yet, many people haven't been given proper spiritual tools, so we tend to come into agreement with and bow down to unhealthy thoughts that God desires us to cast down (2 Corinthians 10:5). This means that these circumstances, experiences, and other people have taken hold in the center of your heart and mind where God should be. Our circumstances, experiences, and interactions with others should not determine whether we deserve to be here; God created you and brought you here, so you have a purpose in being alive: "Before I formed you in the womb I knew you, before you were born I set you apart" (Jeremiah 1:5).

It's not easy to receive the thought that suicide can be associated with idolatry, but I stand as having lived in and through that pit of despair. As God revealed himself to me, it became clear that every reason I attempted to use as a justification to take my own life was allowed to grow within me because I placed those justifications at my heart's center, where God is meant to be. I was not taking those evil thoughts captive or submitting them to Jesus Christ in accordance with 2 Corinthians 10:5. When I was afraid to continue living, I realized I was idolizing and dwelling on the thoughts I perceived other humans had about me. When I felt empty, regardless of my success, I realized I had placed my success as the standard, and at the center of my heart, instead of God. It is time to realize that you may be centering other mindsets and thought patterns in your heart and using those deeply rooted ideologies to justify your existence.

Ask the Holy Spirit to reveal every place in your heart that is centered on other things. Identifying our idolatry tends to be the hardest part of the healing process because it requires an honest evaluation of what we're holding onto, which God needs us to release. While this may be the hardest part, it is also the most freeing, because you will finally release everything that doesn't satisfy, creating space for the God who does. Many feel empty because they have submitted to idols that they thought would bring them peace. Money, social status, and everything we think we've worked for cannot bring the wholeness and peace that your heart is desperately seeking... only God can do that.

Suicide is Shaped by Our Experiences

Your life experiences may have triggered the spirit of suicide. During my experience with my toxic boss, I felt so alone, and the situation felt hopeless. I would come home from work every day feeling defeated, as if no one was listening to me about what I was going through, and as if no one else could comprehend the depth of his impact on the soldiers and the unit... but God heard me. I relied on God because His grace was the only substance that offered me the capacity to continue executing my job. Amid my depression, anxiety, and suicidal thoughts, I was still managing the deployment and redeployment of soldiers across Europe, involving over ten million dollars of government property spread across multiple continents! This circumstance revealed the parts of me that needed God's direct intervention. I had idolized this commander to the point that I allowed his thoughts and comments to drag me to a place of hopelessness.

In my scramble to be heard, I began operating from a spirit of murmuring, complaining, and gossip. This was also one of the most significant sanctification projects God orchestrated in my young life, and I eventually came to recognize the extent of my sin. As a way of escape, I ran to unhealthy and unequal friendships, and I tried numbing my pain with alcohol or men. God brought me to the revelation that I couldn't hold on to these things. He moved in a way that allowed me to no longer be under the toxic commander's leadership, who was eventually fired. To clarify, God has not directed His children to physically remain in toxic situations. It doesn't matter who the human is. If you are in a physically, mentally, and/or emotionally abusive situation, take the earliest opportunity to leave. God's light is called to be separate from the enemy's darkness (2 Corinthians 6:17).

I share this story to declare that God used my difficult circumstances to reveal His heart and hand to me. In my anger and pain toward the situation, I allowed my circumstances to drag me to the pit of despair, and I desired to die. But when I finally submitted my circumstances to the Lord, He changed my situation, heart, and perspective so that I could see His protection and covering through it all.

I pose that some may be suicidal, specifically because of the hardships are facing. I encourage you to ask the Holy Spirit for a renewed perspective. Our hardships can be considered a form of joy only because God is with us in them, and through them, He's providing us with opportunities for growth and insight into our enemy and ourselves (James 1:2-4). God uses our hardships to reveal the true nature of what's inside our hearts, to fortify us, and to remind us that we can only ever lean on Him. God then uses all the revealed information to transform us. Eventually, the things that the enemy uses to gain access to your heart will no longer work because of God's sanctification and healing in those areas of your life.

I must also address those who were severely hurt, whether emotionally, physically, or spiritually, by another person who had a significant role in the hardships they experienced. It's important not to jump to justify any hate, unhealthy actions, or numbing mechanisms because of your circumstances.

In my experience with my toxic boss, I believed I was justified in my complaining and reliance on alcohol and men. While the world may have justified my actions, they were not justified in God's eyes. Moreover, my behavior was self-destructive and only opened doors to shame and guilt that paved the way for suicide. I had to learn the importance of submitting my heart and life to God to be rid of sin, so that God could fight for me. Psalm 66:17-18 states, "I cried out to him with my mouth; his praise was on my tongue. If I had cherished sin in my heart, the Lord would not have listened." Luke 6:27-28 says, "Love your enemies, do good to those who hate you, bless those who curse you, pray for those who mistreat you." I want to clarify that loving your enemies does not mean that you ignorantly accept a toxic individual back into your life. Loving your enemies puts you in a position to be right with God so He can fight on your behalf. It opens your heart to be free from bitterness and teaches you how to entrust things to God instead of engaging in self-destructive behavior.

I must admit that this was one of my hardest lessons, but my heart truly began to shift when I started praying for the person who hurt me most. Dark spirits like resentment, bitterness, and rage were no longer allowed to dwell when I prayed for my enemies. I no longer found comfort in old numbing mechanisms and self-destructive patterns. Allowing our difficult experiences with mean people to justify resenting ourselves and numbing ourselves through toxic behaviors only harms us and the temple that God was meant to dwell in: "In him, you too are being built together to become a dwelling in which God lives by his Spirit" (Ephesians 2:22). Since light and darkness cannot mix, we must allow God's light to shine in those dark places of our hearts so that the darkness brought upon us by our experiences is overcome by the light (2 Corinthians 6:14). Your hardship, no matter what, and I truly mean no matter what it is, can be used by God!

I can admit that many times, I didn't feel like I was changing or experiencing healing, but I was, and I did. Some of you may have been praying and fighting in the spirit and have yet to see your bondage break into the physical realm of your life. I want to encourage you that many of the evil spirits you are breaking have had strongholds over your family for generations, potentially for hundreds of years. These are ancient spirits that will not bow down without a fight. Trust that a war is being waged in the spiritual realm on your behalf, even if you cannot see it. Daniel prayed for three weeks until an angel revealed himself to him. It turned out that the angel was dispatched to assist as soon as Daniel began praying on day one. However, the angel couldn't execute Daniel's prayer until he defeated the enemy that had raged against Daniel in the spiritual realm (Daniel 10). You may not feel anything is happening. Trust that as soon as you commit to seeking God, He will dispatch His angel armies to fight evil spiritual forces on your behalf that you may not see or understand.

DEPRESSION AND SUICIDAL IDEATIONS IN THE BIBLE

Suicide is a Topic Addressed in the Bible.

This section will explore depression and suicidal ideations in the Bible. My testimony is my own, and it is merely a speck in the myriad of experiences people face. My journey led to a discovery of suicide's patterns based on the accounts of those who experienced it in the Bible.

Christians have done a poor job of discussing suicide in church and counseling sessions. We tend to simplify the conversation by saying, "Don't kill yourself because it's a sin," without understanding the underlying roots that are contributing to the spirit of suicide in people's lives. We must get to the heart of the issue with grace and compassion, especially for the families who have suffered loss in this area.

To protect the hearts of those who have experienced losing a loved one from this tragic event, as well as those currently suffering from severe ideations, I will not discuss the suicides that occurred in the Bible (please see Additional Resources for the scriptural references for those who would like to do further reading). Instead, this book will recount the experiences of people who experienced depression or suicidal ideations but were renewed by God. This section aims to provide biblical context to God's ability to restore you in this area and to shed light on what you may be facing. Consider the stories in this section and ask the Holy Spirit to lead you to a revelation about the underlying causes of the spirit of suicide in your life.

Depression in the Bible

Consider the stories of individuals in the Bible who chose life. They continued living with a new perspective because they allowed God to change their hearts. We should consider their stories and learn from their strategies. This section will address the following depressive episodes:

1. Jonah – Jonah 4:8
2. Peter – Various scriptures
3. Paul – 2 Corinthians 1:8-9

Prophet Elijah is also a great example to consider, but I will not address his experiences here, as a portion of his story is shared in the previous "What is the Spirit of Suicide" section. Please read 1 Kings 17-19 and 2 Kings 1-2 to learn more about Elijah.

Jonah was originally in opposition to God's instructions. God wanted to use Jonah to speak to the people of Nineveh because He desired that they have the opportunity to repent, turn away from their sins, and return to Him. However, Jonah didn't want to go to Nineveh and didn't want to be used by God to help those people. Like many of us, Jonah tried to run away from his purpose.

When Jonah went to a different location that God did not approve of, in His mercy, God provided Jonah with a fish to carry him through the sea. God used the fish to put Jonah back on track to address the people of Nineveh. Even after this miracle, Jonah was ungrateful and angry because he still didn't want to speak to the people in Nineveh. In Jonah's mind, he knew that God was gracious, and he didn't think that it was fair for God to try to warn people whom Jonah felt should have been condemned.

Jonah did not want to be used by God to reach people he thought God should punish. Eventually, Jonah obeyed God and went to Nineveh, but he didn't believe God should have sent him there. Jonah was so angry about his situation that he wanted to die: "Now, Lord, take away my life, for it is better for me to die than to live" (Jonah 4:3).

Jonah, like many of us, was also swayed by his ever-changing emotions to the point of desiring death. In Jonah's anger, God was still merciful toward him and caused a tree to grow, providing him with shade to ease his discomfort, which ultimately brought him happiness. The next day, however, God sent a worm to destroy that tree, which made Jonah grow weary. In the heat of the day and in his anger, Jonah again said that "it would be better for me to die than to live" (Jonah 4:8), and he was "so angry [he] wish[ed] [he] were dead" (Jonah 4:9).

Jonah's story ends with God reminding him that He is sovereign, and He alone knows exactly what people need. Jonah was so emotionally charged about the tree, which he had no part in growing, and about the 120,000 people whom he didn't think needed God's word. However, the same compassion God showed Jonah in his anger is the same compassion God extended to the 120,000 people that Jonah preached to but didn't want to reach.

Jonah was so angry that God wanted to use him to show compassion toward others in need of God's word that it made him want to die. Jonah's story is powerful, especially for those who struggle with using their emotions like anger, bitterness, jealousy, and a lack of compassion toward others to justify why they deserve to die. Many of us are like Jonah: we want our lives to look a certain way, and we're angry that God is pushing us down a path that we absolutely cannot stand. We look at the lives of others and are frustrated at what it seems God is doing in their lives, but we're mad that God allowed us to go through certain fire. When you're busy looking at how God has shown up for others, it can be challenging to understand how God has mercifully and graciously shown up for you. God had to rebuke Jonah, and Jonah had to choose to receive the rebuke for his heart to change. We must accept God's correction when he feeds it to us.

Just as God was concerned for Nineveh, God was concerned for Jonah. He provided *a fish* in the ocean to carry Jonah to his purpose. Jonah was so blinded by his anger that he couldn't see what God was doing for him and *through* him for others. God is not a zero-sum God; He can bless you and others simultaneously. You may feel that God is taking you the long way around, and because of your difficult journey, you are ready to give up to the point of death. I pray that you receive the fact that just as God used Jonah, God is using you to reach people with your story, bringing them out of the darkness you will one day fully walk through. Please do not let your fleeting emotions, which are here one day and gone the next, be your justification for ending it all. Choose life by giving God space to correct your broken perspectives and emotions. May you see His compassion and mercy over your life in all things, even in your current situation.

Peter was one of Jesus' twelve disciples who held the honor of learning directly from Him. Peter, who was originally named Simon, received his new name after recognizing that Jesus was the Messiah. In Matthew 16:18, Jesus states, "I tell you that you are Peter, and on this rock I will build my church." Peter was known as what we would call a "ride or die" friend today. He was a loyal leader of the group who had a heart to do right by his rabbi. However, during Jesus' last supper with the disciples, and right before He was arrested to be crucified, Jesus predicted that Peter would deny knowing Him (Matthew 26:33-35; Mark 14:29-31; Luke 22:33-34; John 13:36-38). During dinner, Peter claimed that he would never deny his master.

Following Jesus at this time was very dangerous. The religious leaders wanted to crucify Jesus and do harm to the disciples for sharing that God sent Jesus to save people from their sins. Jesus shared numerous times that He would be betrayed and would suffer horrific things to save God's people, but when what Jesus prophesied came to pass, most of those who were loyal to Him chose to flee out of fear for what could happen to them. When Jesus was betrayed by another disciple named Judas and arrested for His teachings, the disciples deserted Him and fled (Mark 14:50). Yet, Peter followed Jesus at a distance.

As Peter followed his master, he encountered three people who remembered seeing him following Jesus. When asked if he was Jesus' disciple, Peter denied his association with Jesus three times, just as Jesus had prophesied. After realizing what he had done, Peter was filled with sorrow and wept bitterly (Luke 22:60-62). Peter, Jesus' loyal follower, was now filled with shame, guilt, and sorrow, as he watched his savior being led to His death right as he denied ever knowing Him. Like Peter, many have found themselves in a pit of despair due to the accumulation of shame, guilt, and sorrow that seems to have no hope of change.

Yet, the good news is that through His crucifixion, Jesus defeated death, hell, and the grave, and He resurrected after three days to prove that He had power over what seemed like the end of the story. When Jesus resurrected, He revealed Himself to the disciples and had a personal encounter with Peter. John 21:15-25 recounts Jesus' restoration of Peter's assignment as a key leader in the establishment of the early church. Jesus asked Peter three times if he loved Him, and each time Peter responded with his "yes," Jesus charged Peter to "feed [His] sheep," indicating his duty to lead and teach God's people. Jesus' actions show His restorative power. For the three times Peter had previously denied Him, Jesus gave Peter three opportunities to remember his love for Jesus and to remember his purpose. In other words, Jesus replaced Peter's shame, guilt, and sorrow from denying Him with a reminder of love and a charge to keep moving forward with Him.

Peter's story is one of restoration. He's proof that even denying God in a season doesn't keep God from lovingly pursuing and restoring you today. For those who are full of sorrow and despair and aren't running to God because of fear that you've done too much wrong for him to restore you, let the revelation of Peter's story hit your heart. Choose life by allowing God to restore the dark and broken parts of your heart. Every dark thing that is brought to the light becomes restored. God uses these restored places as part of your earthly assignment to help His people.

Paul was a devoted apostle who traveled the world to share the gospel. He's responsible for authoring much of the New Testament. He sacrificed everything he had to tell the world about Jesus, which made him face much suffering. He states:

"We do not want you to be uninformed, brothers and sisters, about the troubles we experienced in the province of Asia. We were under great pressure, far beyond our ability to endure, so that we despaired life itself" (2 Corinthians 1:8).

Paul and his crew faced so much persecution from the world that they did not want to live. Paul continues by saying:

"Indeed, we felt like we had received the sentence of death. But this happened that we might not rely on ourselves but on God, who raises the dead. He has delivered us from such a deadly peril, and he will deliver us again" (2 Corinthians 1:9-10).

Paul exemplifies how believers should hope to respond throughout their sanctification process. When we can acknowledge our suffering, especially when the world's torment brings it about, but still have full faith and confidence that God is fulfilling His will through us, we will no longer stay in bondage to our pain. Paul knew his purpose and that God would keep him alive until he had fulfilled it. Thus, no matter the circumstance, Paul held on to God's promises.

Paul's experience shows that there is a despair that exists, not from sin but because of its absence. Paul was so passionate about the Lord that the world absolutely hated him and devised ways to make him suffer. The difference between this type of despair and any other type of depression is that God's hope, sustaining strength, and unexplainable peace come upon those who fight with God and for His purposes. You might face despair because you fight so diligently for the Lord that the world and its evil principalities are utterly against you. For this population, I encourage you to take heart in Paul's example and trust that God has already overcome the world! The Lord has ordained your steps for the completion of your mission.

Suicide Attempts

This section will address a person who attempted suicide but received salvation because he opened his heart to accept someone else's testimony. We should pay close attention to the power that another person's experience has in displaying the love of Christ. This section will explore the following suicide attempt:

1. The keeper of the prison – Acts 16:20-35 (KJV)

The keeper of the prison was a Roman guard who was responsible for all prisoners under his charge. Paul and Silas, who were preaching the Gospel of Jesus Christ across Rome, were imprisoned for delivering a girl from an evil spirit. Paul and Silas were beaten, jailed, and placed under the responsibility of the keeper of the prison. That evening, Paul and Silas prayed and worshipped the

Lord; their prayer and worship led to an earthquake that shook the prison, opened all the doors, and broke the chains off all the prisoners! Thus, the prisoners could run away if they wanted to, for God had delivered them.

Upon realizing that the prisoners were loose, the Bible declares that the keeper of the prison "drew his sword and was about to kill himself because he thought the prisoners had escaped" (Acts 16:27). The keeper would have killed himself because if the prisoners had escaped, the Roman government would have more than likely held him responsible for the prisoners' escape and punished him severely. In this circumstance, the keeper of the prison faced extreme fear and believed that the best way to rid himself of facing his government's consequences was to take his own life. Most may not be facing consequences from the government, but many are bound to fears that convince them that taking their life is the only way out.

However, the Bible says, "Paul cried out in a loud voice, saying, don't harm yourself! We are all here!" (Acts 16:28). Paul and the prisoners had every right and ability to leave, yet they graciously stayed behind. Paul used this experience to witness to the keeper of the prison about Jesus. The keeper fell to his face before Paul and Silas, overwhelmed by awe and gratitude for their mercy and for what their God had done to deliver them. He asked them what he had to do to be saved. Paul and Silas read the keeper of the prison the Word of God, baptized him, and rejoiced with him for his salvation.

This experience is such a reflection of Christ's love for us. Many are representatives of the keeper of the prison. God's grace toward us is shown through His children, especially when we don't feel we deserve it, and these reflections of His light lead us straight to Him. Many have attempted suicide out of extreme fear of life's circumstances. Let this story serve as an example: fear is a thief of your peace and your ability to see anything beyond it. There are probably people in your life who are trying to speak life into you, declaring the name of Jesus over you, and who desire to see you walk with God; don't ignore them. Allow them to reflect God's love toward you and receive God's grace. May a healthy community be there for you in your time of need.

HOW TO FIGHT

For those who are led by the Spirit of God are the children of God. The Spirit you received does not make you slaves, so that you live in fear again; rather, the Spirit you received brought about your adoption to sonship. And by him we cry, "Abba, Father."

The Spirit himself testifies with our spirit that we are God's children.

Now if we are children, then we are heirs – heirs of God and co-heirs with Christ, if indeed we share in his sufferings in order that we may also share in his glory.

Romans 8: 14-17

How to Fight!

It's time to recognize that you are Abba-Father's beloved child and heir. As an heir, you have access to his promises of unconditional love, forgiveness, constant access to His presence, and an eternal inheritance. Thus, it is time to fight alongside Him, knowing you have the best daddy in the world who is interested in seeing you live and thrive with the time He's given you on earth.

The entirety of this book has established your understanding of the supernatural nature of suicide, as well as God's intention against it. By now, your understanding of how the spiritual world operates has increased; you can recognize what the spirit of suicide is and how it may have been allowed to operate in your life. Moreover, you have parts of my testimony and stories from the Bible itself to showcase examples of all the patterns discussed. We are now at the phase of this journey where you will learn how to fight and defeat the spirit of suicide!

Belief

We must first start from a place of belief. The Bible says that if we have faith the size of a mustard seed, we can move mountains (Matthew 17:20). Many may believe that God can do it for someone else, but struggle to believe He can do it for them. You have a great and mighty God who is ready to back you when you choose Him, and He's so big that the clouds are like dust to His feet (Nahum 1:3). Pick up a speck of dust on your floor and hold it up to your eye; *that* is how small the vast clouds in the sky are to God! God is magnificent enough to handle any problem and help you break it. Jesus himself spoke that "everything is possible for one who believes" (Mark 9:23). Now is the time to stretch your faith.

I acknowledge that some may still question whether freedom can be their portion. I encourage this population to take note of a father in the Bible who asked Jesus to heal his child in bondage to an evil spirit. This father told Jesus that he believed, but he honestly asked Jesus to help him overcome his unbelief (Mark 9:24)! Take a moment to ask the Lord to help you overcome your unbelief, then open your heart to accept what God can and will do for you.

Salvation

While reading this book, many will have felt the tug of the Holy Spirit in their hearts. For those who do not know Jesus but feel led to come to Him, you can, at this moment, accept Him into your heart. You don't have to have an altar call or a public encounter. God can move in whatever way He needs to get your attention to come to Him, so if He's pulling you toward Him, don't deny that call. Just accept Him. The Bible says that if you confess with your mouth that Jesus is Lord and believe in your heart that God raised him from the dead, you will be saved (Romans 10:9). To be clear, a prayer is not the thing that leads to your salvation; salvation is you choosing to accept and submit to Jesus Christ in all your ways. Moreover, there is no one way to pray for God to hear you. Jesus provides the ultimate prayer template in Matthew 6:9-13 that I encourage all to dwell in. For those feeling the desire to run to God for salvation, sanctification, and eternal life, but are unsure of how to respond, you may pray the provided prayer with me:

God,

I humbly come before you, acknowledging you as my Lord. Thank you for creating me, loving me, and tugging on my heart. I believe that you sent your son Jesus to die and rise again for my sins so that I could be set free. I repent for and renounce my relationship with all my sins (confess all your sins to him now); I replace them with the blood of Jesus Christ and declare my freedom in you. Father, thank you for my salvation. I receive your gifts of love, forgiveness, and redemption. Please lead me on this journey of sanctification, closer to you.

In Jesus' Name. Amen.

Sanctification

If you accepted Jesus as your Lord and Savior, congratulations! All of heaven is rejoicing at your decision. The word says that when we are with Christ, we are a new creation; the old is gone, and the new is here (2 Corinthians 5:17). Thus, you must begin to walk by faith in your newness. This is known as the sanctification process, and it requires that you submit all of yourself to God so that He can strip away every foundation that was not built on Him.

The sanctification process is a lifetime process, and every experience you face from now on is part of it. Grab a Bible and learn God's word to grow your relationship with Him. Ask Him to reveal Himself through His word.

Submitting to safe and true Godly leaders within a local church and/or community is also essential. Not everyone who claims the Christian title is truly walking with God; thus, it is important to discern who is shepherding God's children and who is merely a wolf in sheep's clothing. Ask God to strengthen your discernment and trust what He reveals to you. You will not be perfect. None of us are, but it's okay. The goal throughout this lifetime is to walk with God's love and authority and to reflect Christ's character in every aspect of our lives.

Let me be clear: salvation is the first step for anyone not in Christ, but it is not the only step. Whether you are newly saved or have been saved for some time, we must all undergo the process of sanctification. Churches typically prioritize and focus on salvation without giving the body of Christ the tools necessary to understand sanctification. I say this because so many people who have claimed to have received Christ are still in bondage because they haven't been taught to fully submit to the process of Christ changing them. The point isn't to become saved and then continue to stay in bondage. God doesn't just want to offer you eternal life; He's so kind that He desires to give you a life full of freedom while living on earth, too. Come to Christ as you are, receive your salvation, and allow Him to sanctify you through your life experiences so that you walk in His freedom and grow to become more like Him.

If you are reading this book, you have more than likely been battling with the spirit of suicide for a long time, strictly because no one has taught you how to go through life fighting against evil things in the spiritual realm. Many have questioned whether God can deliver you because you have walked with Christ for some time, but are still tormented by this evil spirit. I suggest that we shouldn't limit our relationship with Christ to only experiencing His promises in eternity; the Lord desires that we learn to walk in freedom now, while we are on earth. Thus, freedom from suicide requires that we submit to Him to change us as *He* sees fit. God needs you to give Him full access to uproot the heart postures, the emotions, and the people you've held onto for so long, so that you can heal and be free.

Create Space

The process the Lord brought me through to heal from suicidal ideations and depression that I now share with you is a biblical blueprint. However, I want to be clear that God can and will move in your life as He desires, and my process is not the only way to be healed. We're talking about the same God who offered eternal life to the criminal who was being crucified on a cross next to Jesus simply because he had faith in Him (Luke 23:32-43). This man didn't live a lifetime following Jesus; he could count the remaining minutes of his life, yet the Lord offered him freedom. Some people receive immediate healing through Jesus' touch, as seen in the case of the woman with the issue of blood (Luke 8:43-48). Some people receive healing through a process, like the man born blind (John 9:1-12) or Lazarus being raised from the dead (John 11:38-44). The central theme across all of Jesus' healings is that the people He healed all chose to come; they operated with the faith that He could heal them, and God received the glory. In other words, those who decide to go to Him and have faith in Him will be set free and reveal God's glory to others through their testimony.

    I'm addressing this because we need to create space for God to move in our lives miraculously. As people who are accustomed to operating with depression and suicidal ideations, time isn't typically a friend. The beautiful thing about God is that He sits outside of time. As we submit ourselves to the belief that God can heal, we must also give God space to surprise us.

    It is true that when it comes to dealing with issues within our hearts, the Lord may require a process to address and resolve those issues. Numerous lessons in the Bible demonstrate that God will strengthen our faith, trust, and patience in seasons that require us to wait. However, just because you invested a certain amount of time in pain doesn't mean that the Lord must take that *same amount* of time to heal you. We typically hear the phrase that "healing takes time." Please do not strictly adopt a phrase and continue to speak something over your life that is not *always* true, based on Jesus' example. I say this because my testimony was full of restoration, just as I trust many of yours will be, and many times God's restoration comes faster than we think.

    In 2022, I received a prophetic word from Joel 2:25, which states that the Lord will restore to us what the locusts have stolen. At that phase of my life, I was steeped in an ungodly relationship that the Lord told me to get out of. I was engaged in fornication, adultery, idolatry, and many other sins that kept me in bondage to suicide and depression. It felt like there was no hope. When I finally turned back to God to allow him to mold me in 2023, I was free from suicidal ideations and depression within three months, was engaged to my childhood sweetheart in four months, and married to him as my kingdom-ordained spouse in nine months from the time I fully recommitted to Christ – ten years of pain restored in nine months. I say this not to compare timelines, but to offer you hope. When God needs you to be in a particular position, He will restore you to that position.

Let me be *very* clear: this is not a "get healed quick" doctrine, and my story is not complete. The Lord continues to expose the issues of my heart that must be addressed, and the devil is busy at work trying to dismantle God's plans. However, because I have experienced God's restorative nature, I now have the faith and confidence to fight *from* victory as I face life's challenges that are bound to arise. I share this portion of my testimony to free some who believe God *only* responds after significant amounts of time. Let God show up for you in whatever way He needs to, for His glory.

The "4 R's"

The devil is so sneaky that he wants you to believe that obtaining freedom is too difficult or complicated for *you* to do, and I am here to offer the hope that it's not. Your liberty is obtainable with Christ. I'm not promising that you won't experience human emotions or challenging experiences as you begin to pursue freedom. I warn that as you start to heal and be free, the devil will more than likely raise his head in an attempt to get you back into the very bondage you're trying to leave. You must take your stand against the devil's schemes and stand firm in the word of God, and in His whole armor (Ephesians 6:10-20).

One of your most potent weapons against the enemy is your voice. When you declare scriptures and prayers out of your mouth, you declare them for God to hear and for your heart to receive. Thus, to break any and every evil spirit off your life associated with suicide or any other spirit, you must open your mouth to repent, renounce, replace, and receive (Montgomery, 27- 44). We must repent for our sins, renounce and break any covenants with evil things, replace them with the name and blood of Jesus Christ, and receive God's forgiveness and love.

2 Chronicles 7:14 states, "If my people, who are called by my name, will humble themselves and pray and seek my face and turn from their wicked ways, then I will hear from heaven and I will forgive their sin and heal their land." This powerful scripture is our blueprint to freedom. If we humble ourselves before God, pray and seek Him, and repent for our sins, He will forgive, heal, and restore us!

Repent

In my 18+ years of going to church, I was never taught how to live a lifestyle of repentance. Like many, I believed that once I repented during my salvation prayer, I would never have to do it again, because that prayer would cover me for the rest of my life. However, this journey taught me that because I am human and fall short of His glory, I must repent to rid myself of the weight of sin. Repentance is simply the act of turning away. It's confessing the entire truth about our hearts, motives, and actions to God. Repentance requires action; it should not be an empty and false apology with no intention of turning away from the sin. The Holy Spirit will first give your heart a conviction. The Lord's love for you, coupled with your love and reverence for Him, will then guide you away from unhealthy behaviors and toward Godly ones.

Some may question why they must repent when evil things have been done to them. First, our requirement as believers to repent does not clear the other person who hurt you from repentance. The Bible states that we must all give an account on judgment day (Romans 14:12) and that every knee shall bow down to the name of Jesus Christ (Philippians 2:10-11). Someone else's unrepentant evil toward you has already been accounted for and seen by God, and He may already be moving in the natural and eternal realm if they do not repent. But someone else's evil behavior toward us doesn't justify our ability to remain unrepentant toward God. Because just as others have hurt us, there are many ways that each of us has grieved our Father in heaven (Matthew 18:21-35). None of us can afford for God to be unforgiving toward our sins (Romans 6:23). Secondly, repentance purifies our hearts and shows God our humility, and the Lord loves to support and fight for humble servants (Matthew 20:26-28). Lastly, repentance leads to freedom. I noticed that when I repented for the ways that I hurt people and hurt God during my depressed state, *that* was when He freed me from shame and guilt. I was holding on to the laundry list of ways that I hurt people, and people had hurt me, but when I laid it all on God's throne in repentance, it felt like a weight lifted because I was no longer hoarding this list of problems. I challenge that those suffering from suicidal ideations and depression need an intense repentance session where you just lay everything in your heart at the feet of Jesus... and pay attention to how much lighter you feel afterwards... Proverbs 28:13 says, "Whoever conceals their sins does not prosper, but the one who confesses and renounces them finds mercy." The trick of the enemy is to keep you so angry at the people who hurt you that you try to justify why you don't have to repent for the things you're holding onto. And the Bible says that anyone who hides their sins will not prosper! Choose life by repenting for the things you have held onto for so long.

The repentance process can also be applied to your bloodline. To clarify, each is responsible for working out their own salvation (Philippians 2:12). Still, you can intercede and repent for the generational sins and curses that have perpetuated depression and suicidal ideations within your bloodline. Judges 21:6 highlights that the rest of the tribes of Israel repented for their brethren in the tribe of Benjamin, who had brought great sin upon themselves and Israel (KJV). Thus, to walk in freedom, repentance must be a consistent habit for yourself, your family, your nation, and beyond.

It's essential to live a lifestyle of repentance because Jesus died and was resurrected so that we have access to this *free gift*. We cannot hide from God; He already sees everything, and He is a good Father. Allowing our sins to accumulate before we approach God grieves Him, because He desires us to trust Him with the weight of our sins, for which He already has a solution. He loves you so much that He wants you to take advantage of His gift of repentance so that He can also freely offer His forgiveness. Just like a child who runs straight to their parent in tears after falling in the playground, the Lord desires for us to run straight to Him when we've fallen and need help… and He is there with open arms to receive you in His love. Just like the good parent with their child, God will give you a big kiss and a lollipop as He solves your problems.

Renounce

To renounce means to break a covenant with something. Breaking a covenant means that you are coming out of a serious, law-binding agreement. When fighting the spirit of suicide, remember that suicide is like the rotten fruit on a tree that has many roots. This means that you may be in a covenant, not only with suicide but also with each root from the suicide tree. Thus, you must formally renounce all known and unknown covenants that are contributing to suicide and depression in your life. As you begin to pray and repent, ensure you are also formally renouncing every covenant associated with the roots of suicide and depression. You may even say, "I renounce the spirit of suicide and all its roots," – and name all the roots that you can think of, as well as any others the Lord brings to your attention (such as shame, guilt, silence, idolatry, rejection, etc.).

Renouncing serves as a powerful warfare tactic because it serves as your declaration that you are forsaking the previously long-standing hold that the devil had over you. It's you saying, "devil, I've had enough, and I'm no longer in agreement with your schemes; I'm going to be choosing differently." It is essential that as you renounce with your mouth, you back it up with your actions. For example, if one of your "suicide roots" is anger, then when placed in a situation where you would typically respond in anger, intentionally choose to respond with patience instead. Your words, backed by your actions, demonstrate to the enemy that he is losing the foothold that initially gave him access to you.

If you're someone who continues to be plagued by suicide and depression after attempting to pray, I encourage you to consider adding renouncement declarations to your prayers. Evil covenants don't end because the bloodline forgot, didn't speak about them, or didn't know they were there. They end when a person arises to formally end the relationship with them through the blood of Jesus. You must end that evil covenant with suicide and depression by formally renouncing it *and its roots* with the words out of your mouth, and then backing up your words with different actions.

Our inability to come out of agreement with the roots associated with suicide is one of the main reasons the spirits related to suicide continue to run rampant over time. You may already be praying powerful words like, "I rebuke the spirit of suicide," or, "I cast the spirit of suicide into the abyss." While these are compelling phrases, the spirit's removal will only be temporary if the covenant or relationship with the evil spirit and its roots are still intact. In other words, we can pray against depression all we want. Still, if we choose to continue to remain in depressed situations, lifestyles, and relationships, it will be unrealistic to expect freedom. We must back our declarations with faith through our actions.

I want to be clear that the fight against suicide isn't about *you striving* to be a different person who makes different decisions. It's about *you relying* on Jesus' strength to take the steps *He asks you to* take in obedience. When we take a single step in obedience, the Lord will respond to our faith supernaturally. As you take one step, He will continue to push you to take another, and one day, you'll look back and realize that you've hiked an entire mountain trail with Him. He'll no longer have to push you to step because your knowledge of His love for you and your love for Him will inspire you to continue walking with Him in every area of your life.

Replace

The truth is, when you begin to repent and renounce, you've just made the devil very upset because he realizes he is no longer able to hold you down like he used to. Thus, all those evil spirits that were lying dormant and at rest, and were keeping you in bondage, are going to begin to get mad. They are scared because they know their time in your life is almost up; they're about to get evicted from their house. They will want to do everything in their power to retaliate so that they can stay.

Keep in mind that when you renounce, you are breaking a covenant, and as we continue to discuss, covenants are a big deal in the spiritual realm. To simplify the concept, I will speak as if a covenant is a contract.

Imagine that you entered a contract. Let's say you entered this contract with evil and bad people. When you partnered initially with these evil people, you didn't know how terrible they were because they seemed nice. Now that you are aware that they are bad people, you know you must get out of this contract. However, you cannot simply break a contract without facing the legally binding consequences outlined in the contract.

Now replace every word "contract" in the example above with the word "covenant," and replace the word "people" with "spirit." This is how evil covenants work. Once you break an evil covenant by renouncing it, there's a price, a consequence, or a ransom that must be paid. This is where replacing comes in.

Replacing means to offer something else instead. In the case of evil covenants, you cannot stop at renouncing the evil covenant. Otherwise, these awakened evil spirits are going to continue to come after you because you've just upset them with the broken covenant. They originally had the spiritually legal right to stay in your life because of whatever the people who hurt you, members of your bloodline, or you were doing. We ask the question, "God, why is this stuff happening to me?" Many times, it is because a person (whether you, someone in your bloodline, or the people who hurt you) unknowingly gave the devil legal spiritual access to enter and take over through sinful behavior. Other times, it is because the enemy recognizes your righteousness and is trying to take you off God's course. No matter what, anything that happens in your life can be restored by the Lord and display His glory when you choose Him.

To explain further, let's consider the spirit of anger again. If one of your "suicide roots" is anger, and you simply renounce the spirit of anger from your life, the spirit of anger that has probably been peacefully resting with you and your family for a long time may start raging within you even more. He rages because he can no longer hide. He knows that *you know* he's there, and he wants to do everything in his power not to get evicted from the home he's known for so long. Thus, simply renouncing him only wakes him up so that he can begin testing the terms of your contract (covenant). Without anything to challenge this spirit, he will more than likely come back stronger than before. Matthew 12:43-

45 clarifies that "when an impure spirit comes out of a person, it goes through arid places seeking rest and does not find it. Then it says, 'I will return to the house I left.' When it arrives, it finds the house unoccupied, swept clean and put in order. Then it goes and takes with it seven other spirits more wicked than itself, and they go in and live there. And the final condition of that person is worse than the first."

Thus, replacing is a necessary component of your warfare toolkit because it's not enough just to be temporarily free from the evil spirits associated with suicide and depression. Those spirits will come back to snatch your newfound freedom if the house they originally dwelled in is empty and void of the *power* of the Holy Spirit. Every covenant we renounce must be replaced with something more potent in its stead so that evil spirits no longer have the right to wreak havoc in our lives. The only viable ransom able to stand in place of your broken covenants is the name and blood of Jesus Christ. To replace, you may say something to the effect of, "I replace every broken evil covenant in my life with the name and blood of Jesus Christ."

Many Christians have been filled with doubt because they identify as Christian, are very depressed or suicidal, and have questioned whether the Holy Spirit is in them because of their mental health struggles. I want to offer the hope that Jesus hasn't left you because of your struggles. As a matter of fact, He wants you to lean on Him, and He loves you *with* (not in spite of) your struggles. We have a choice of which authority we give more power to. When replacing, it's essential to remember that Jesus is the most powerful, and the evil coming against you is insignificant by comparison. In my journey, even though I knew I housed the Holy Spirit inside me while feeling suicidal and depressed, I was so discouraged because it didn't *feel like* the Holy Spirit was there. I could still hear his voice; I could still hear him calling me, but I had given more *power and authority* to the enemy in my head and heart instead of God.

As Christians, we are called to partner *with* Christ in His work, and our role in this process involves *dwelling in and resting in* the power and authority of Jesus, recognizing that His power is exponentially greater than the devil's.

I acknowledge that even understanding that God is powerful can be immensely challenging when the heaviness of death feels so imminent. What aided me was consuming scriptures that re-focused my heart and mind on the power and love of God (refer to the scriptures in Additional Resources). When I began to capture the love God had for me in my heart, the strength that the enemy seemed to have over me dwindled. As I replaced everything with the blood of Jesus, the spirit of death that dwelled on the inside of me had no choice but to become light: "But everything exposed by the light becomes visible – and everything that is illuminated becomes a light" (Ephesians 5:13).

As a warning, do not replace any evil covenant with any other person's name besides the name of Jesus. If you declare any other person's name besides Jesus, you will be positioning another human to stand in your stead in these evil covenants (which is witchcraft). The only person who can stand in your place because He already defeated death, hell, and the grave is Jesus Christ!

As you begin to declare the name and blood of Jesus, you may be faced with spiritual warfare. I want to encourage you that this is normal! These evil spirits are terrified for their lives because they know they are about to be expelled. They are trying to intimidate you to stop fighting by bombarding you with attacks. Remain focused on and rested in God's love for you, persistent in your prayers and declaration of the scriptures, and consider fasting.

Matthew 17:21 (KJV) says that there are certain things that can only be addressed through prayer and fasting. In my pursuit of freedom from suicide and depression, I chose to fast. When fasting, we choose to rely on prayer and scripture as our food. Fasting is a tool that teaches us to grow in our faith, and it moves mountains in the spiritual realm. In a personal experience, I was praying against attacks of regression and delay because it was evident from my dreams that the enemy wanted me to go back to making poor decisions. When I finally chose to fast, God allowed me to see the demon attacking me cower down at the declaration of God's word and the name of Jesus Christ! I remember declaring Philippians 2:10-11, which states "that at the name of Jesus every knee should bow, in heaven and on earth and under the earth, and every tongue acknowledge that Jesus Christ is Lord, to the glory of God the Father." Seeing the entity attacking me cower down at the name of Jesus was all the proof I needed to know that this demonic attack that felt so huge in one season was nothing compared to the blood of Jesus Christ! If I, as someone who used to be terrified to fight evil in the spiritual realm, can do it, you can, too. Continue to replace every evil covenant with the love, blood, and name of Jesus Christ, and watch him work!

Receive

Receiving is a vital part of your prayer process because it ensures you remain grounded in God's love. This section will be invaluable for those who are struggling with repentance and still feel guilt and shame about their past. To receive means to accept freely. As already mentioned, God is a loving God. Moreover, He says that He will forgive and heal us if we repent and turn back to Him (2 Chronicles 7:14).

Many have a difficult time understanding how anyone could freely offer their love and forgiveness after simply bringing their issues to Him. We have tried to force God into our human mold. In our humanness, we've more than likely experienced people who were unforgiving. Moreover, we have also been unforgiving because of the pain others have caused us. Our human experiences have prevented us from experiencing the supernatural, unexplainable, and incomprehensible vastness of God. His ways are not our ways, and His thoughts are not our thoughts (Isaiah 55:8). He promises to forgive our past, and He throws it all away (Jeremiah 31:34; Psalm 103:12). Choosing life requires that we accept God's love, grace, forgiveness, and more.

Part of receiving God's love also involves basking in His rest. I've fought many demonic battles, and some required intense warfare. I've had seasons where I was being called to fast, pray, and meditate on scriptures day and night. These encounters led to powerful breakthroughs in my life. I must honestly acknowledge, though, that the Lord has also taken me through seasons of resting with Him through the fight. These are times when He calls me to practice having childlike joy and to eat and be merry in the middle of oppressive attacks, and these seasons honestly bring more breakthroughs than those requiring intense warfare. Just like Jesus rested during the storm with his disciples, He desires that we rest in Him during our storms (Matthew 8:23-27). Trust that even if it doesn't feel like He's moving, He *is* moving, and He may just be calling you to fight with new strategies. Thus, you must remain attentive to hear how the Lord needs *you* to fight in this season.

All the warring in the world means nothing if we're not able to grasp His freedom in our hearts. Thus, the process of receiving requires that we forgo the logic in our brains for our hearts' sake. The world has more than likely discounted every attempt for you to think with your heart. We pride ourselves on making logical and well-prepared decisions with our brains. With God, however, it's more challenging to comprehend Him with our brains because He doesn't operate the way in which the devil has distorted the world to operate. God has always intended for His love to be received and written on the tablets of our hearts (Proverbs 7:1-3). Thus, when practicing your ability to receive God's love, it's essential to come to Him like a child because, in His eyes, that's exactly who you are to Him. In their attempt to seek greatness, the disciples asked Jesus who was the greatest in the Kingdom of Heaven, and Jesus responded by saying that those who take the humble position of a child are the greatest in God's Kingdom (Matthew 18:1-5). Consider the fact that children who know they are loved embody the most vigorous faith, have magnificent imaginations, and know without a shadow of a doubt that they can ask for and receive what they ask for because of how loved they are.

If you are struggling to receive God's gifts of repentance, forgiveness, or any other gift, consider asking Him to wash you in His love and reveal how He sees you. Submit every ounce of childhood and parental trauma for Him to reframe what may be tainting your ability to see Him as the loving Father He is. He desires to build you on His firm foundation of love so that you know with confidence that the God who created you is genuinely pleased with you and desires to shower you with His love, forgiveness, and compassion as you fight against depression and suicide.

Action

The Lord is not done with you, child of God. His love will become a living well within your heart, encouraging you to choose life each day. Rejoice in each day as a celebration of the steps you have taken with Jesus and rely on your warfare toolkit to combat the wiles of the enemy. Prioritize God's love and make repentance, renouncing, replacing, and receiving part of your lifestyle, and watch how God releases you from suicide's grip. Watch how He changes your heart. Watch how He heals you from the inside out.

As you continue to walk, trust that the Lord will use you to deliver others from similar circumstances. I ask that, in His timing, you share your powerful testimony. Someone else will live simply because you chose life, too.

My prayer is that you walk in the fullness of the life that God gave you. May you see yourself as the wonderfully created being that God intentionally crafted and completely loves. These new spiritual tools are now in your toolkit to supplement your natural resources to combat suicide. You have taken your fight to the next level by fighting suicide in the spiritual realm with Jesus Christ on your side. May your hope in the God who so deeply loves you be restored. I dispatch His angel armies to fight on your behalf.

"Come to me, all who are weary and burdened, and I will give you rest."

Matthew 11:28

Lord, I speak that the bonds of suicide be broken off your children in Jesus' name.

Amen.

ADDITIONAL RESOURCES

Example 4R Prayer

The following example prayer follows the 4R model (repent, renounce, replace, and receive). Please consider this prayer as a base and make it your own:

Thank you, Father, for the gift of repentance. Thank you for offering me a way to confess my sins and struggles in your mercy. Father, I repent for (<u>list every sin</u>). As I repent, I renounce and break the covenant with every evil thing that has allowed suicide and depression to wreak havoc in my life and my bloodline. I declare in accordance with your word in Isaiah 54:17 that no weapon formed against me shall prosper.

As I break these evil covenants, I bind them and cast them into the abyss. Your word says that "whatever you bind on earth will be bound in heaven, and whatever you loose on earth will be loosed in heaven" (Matthew 18:18). Therefore, as I bind those evil spirits on earth, I trust they are bound in the spiritual realm. I loose Jehovah Sabaoth, God of the angel armies, to fight and defeat them on my behalf.

I replace every evil covenant with the blood of Jesus and the name of Jesus Christ. I declare that every evil thing attempting to attack me, every evil idol, and every evil spirit must stand against you. Since the Bible declares that every knee shall bow and every tongue shall confess that Jesus is Lord, every evil thing that has been raging against me must bow down and confess the name of Jesus Christ (Philippians 2:10-11).

Father, I thank you for purifying me and making me more like your Son each day. Thank you for allowing me to accept your forgiveness and walk freely in your freedom. Thank you for throwing my transgressions as far as the East is from the West (Psalm 103:12). Thank you for loving me, and I love you.

In Jesus' name, Amen.

Scriptures to Pray

Etch the scriptures on the tablet of your heart (Proverbs 3:1-3). The scriptures below serve as a starting point to help shape your identity as God's child, understand God's love for you, and develop your warfare strategy. The scriptures provided are not an exhaustive or all-inclusive list. The key is to encourage you to find scriptures that give you the strength and ability to counter the enemy's tactics. Ephesians 6:17 describes the word of God as the sword for our armor; thus, scriptures are a vital part of our spiritual walk.

OLD TESTAMENT	NEW TESTAMENT
Deuteronomy 28:7-10	Romans 5:17
Joshua 1:8	Romans 8
Nehemiah 8:10	Romans 15:13
Job 22:8	1 Corinthians 1:30
Psalm 5:12	1 Corinthians 2:16
Psalm 13:2-4	2 Corinthians 1:20
Psalm 51	2 Corinthians 5:17;21
Psalm 55:22	2 Corinthians 8:9
Psalm 68:19	2 Corinthians 12:9
Psalm 91	Galatians 3:13
Psalm 135:4	Ephesians 1:7
Proverbs 11:31	Ephesians 2:8-13
Proverbs 12:14	Ephesians 3:17;20
Proverbs 16:7	Ephesians 6:10-24
Proverbs 18:20	Philippians 1:6
Isaiah 26:3	Philippians 2:16
Isaiah 55:11	Philippians 3:12-14
Isaiah 60:1	Philippians 4:6-8
Isaiah 62:3-4	Colossians 1:11-13
Jeremiah 23:29	1 Thessalonians 5:16-18
Jeremiah 29:11	2 Thessalonians 3:16
Joel 2:25	2 Timothy 1:7
Zephaniah 3:17	Hebrews 10:35
Zechariah 2:8	Hebrews 11
	1 John 2:1
	1 John 4:17
	3 John 1:3

Scriptures About Suicide

This section includes a list of suicides in the Bible. I caution those who are currently experiencing suicidal ideations to pursue reading these scriptures in the presence of safe, trusted community partners (counselors, pastors, trusted family members, mentors, and close friends). I've included these scriptures so that those who are in positions to aid others experiencing suicidal ideations may receive biblically-based revelations from the Holy Spirit about the nature of suicide.

BIBLE CHARACTER	SCRIPTURE REFERENCE
Abimelek	Judges 9:54
King Saul and his armor-bearer	1 Samuel 31:4-6
Ahithophel	2 Samuel 17:23
Zimri	1 Kings 16:18
Judas	Matthew 27:5

Additional Reading

The following book list provides additional reading that may help aid your understanding of the spiritual realm and God's love for you:

BOOK TITLE	AUTHOR
Abba's Child: The Cry of the Heart for Intimate Belonging	Brennan Manning
Unbroken Curses: Hidden Source of Trouble in the Christian's Life	Rebecca Brown, MD, with Daniel Yoder
Setting the Captives Free	Pastor Bev Tucker
Deliverance from Demonic Covenants and Curses	Reverend James Solomon
Freedom from Soul Wounds and Demons: Your Breakthrough to True Peace and Joy	Nelson L. Schuman
Angel Armies: Releasing the Warriors of Heaven	Tim Sheets

We Want to Hear From You

If you or a loved one experienced God's heart from this book, we want to hear about it. Your testimony is powerful, and we would be honored to receive it. You may share your story and prayer requests via email to:

officialgreenehouse@gmail.com

Seeking More Content?

Subscribe on YouTube @Calli Greene.

Works Cited

Hagin, Kenneth W. "What is Rhema?" Kenneth Hagin Ministries, 2017, What Is Rhema? - Rhema. Accessed 9 July 2025.

Macinnis, Adam. "Study: Trauma-Informed Bible Reading Reduces Depression, Anxiety, Anger." Christianity Today, 2023, https://www.christianitytoday.com/2021/05/bible-reading-study-trauma-ptsd-covid19-mental-health/. Accessed 26 Dec. 2024.

Montgomery, Tiphani. *The Year of the Bride: Supernatural Strategy for Marital Breakthrough*. Covered By God LLC, 2024, pp. 27-44.

Centers for Disease Control and Prevention (CDC). "Suicide Prevention: Risk and Protective Factors for Suicide." Risk and Protective Factors for Suicide | Suicide Prevention | CDC.

The Holy Bible, King James Version. Oxford UP, 1998.

The Holy Bible, New International Version. Biblica, 2011.

www.ingramcontent.com/pod-product-compliance
Lightning Source LLC
Chambersburg PA
CBHW060343170426
43202CB00014B/2867